THE NATURE KIDS GUIDE TO

CHIMPANZEES

DAVID ANDERSON

LP Media Inc. Publishing
Text copyright © 2026 by LP Media Inc.
All rights reserved.

For information address LP Media Inc. Publishing,
30012 Variolite St NW, Princeton MN 55371
www.lpmedia.org

Publication Data

Chimpanzees
The Nature Kid's Guide to Chimpanzees — First edition.

Summary: "Learn all about Chimpanzees, the Nature Kid Way"
— Provided by publisher.

ISBN: 979-8-89818-130-7

[1. Chimpanzees – Non-Fiction] I. Title.

Title: The Nature Kid's Guide to Chimpanzees

CONTENTS

TREETOP HOMES

Chimps never use the same nest twice! They also make day nests for afternoon naps. Baby chimps sleep in their mother's nest until they are about five years old.

Hoot! A chimp sits high in a leafy tree. It watches the forest below.

Chimpanzees live in forests. They spend most of their time in trees. Tall trees give them food and safe places to sleep.

When they need to sleep, chimps build nests to rest in. They bend branches together and add soft leaves on top. This only takes about 5 minutes! They are very skilled builders.

Each night, chimps make a new nest. They pick spots high off the ground – some nests sit 50 feet up!

The forest **canopy** is their home. It has everything they need to survive.

AFRICAN APES

Screech! A chimp swings through vines in Africa. It calls to its family.

Chimpanzees only live in Africa. They are found in 21 different countries, mostly in central and western Africa.

Chimpanzees can live in many habitats. Some live in wet rainforests. Others live in dry grasslands with scattered trees.

Their range once stretched all across Africa. But many forests have been cut down. Today, chimps live in smaller patches of forest.

The Democratic Republic of Congo has more wild chimps than any other country, around 65,000!

8

Thump! A young chimp lands on the ground and stands up tall.

Chimpanzees are about the same size as kids! Adult chimps can stand about 3 to 5.5 feet tall. That is shorter than most grown-ups.

Male chimps weigh about 100 pounds. Females are smaller, weighing around 70 pounds.

Chimps have long arms that reach past their knees. Their arm span can stretch over 5 feet wide! This helps them climb and swing through trees.

A chimp's brain is only one-third the size of a human brain, but they are still very smart!

BUILT TO CLIMB

Grip! A chimp grabs a branch with its strong hand.

Chimpanzees have bodies made for climbing. Their hands have long fingers and short thumbs. This shape helps them grip branches tightly.

Chimp feet work like extra hands! Their big toes stick out to the side. They can grab things with their feet while climbing.

Chimps have strong muscles in their arms and shoulders. These muscles make them about 1.5 times stronger than humans! Their thick, tough bones support all that strength. All these parts work together to help chimps move through trees.

12

Click! A chimp turns its head. It hears a sound far away.

Chimpanzees have sharp senses. Their eyes see colors just like humans do. They can spot ripe fruit in green leaves.

Chimpanzees also have great hearing. They hear higher sounds than humans can. This helps them hear each other's calls in the thick forest.

Their sense of smell is strong too. Chimps sniff food to check if it is safe to eat. They can even recognize family members just by smell!

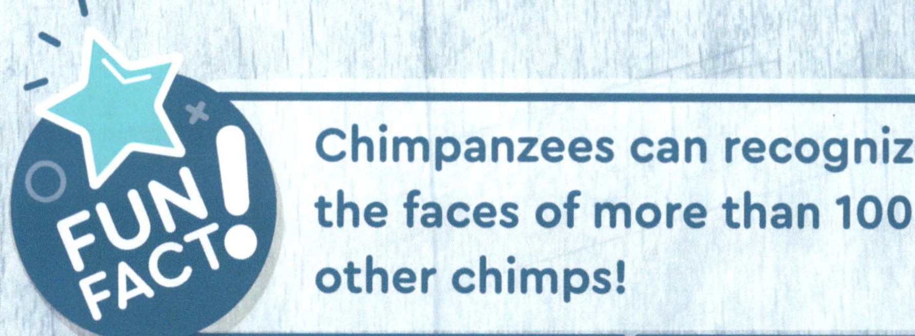

TOUGH
TROOPS

Growl! A big chimp shows its teeth. Others stand close by.

Chimpanzees stay safe by living in groups called **troops**. A troop can have 15 to 150 chimps! With so many members, there is strength in numbers.

Chimps protect each other from danger. When a predator comes near, they make loud calls. This warns the whole troop.

Male chimps guard their territory. They patrol the edges and chase away other chimps. Working together keeps everyone safe.

Chimps will throw rocks and sticks at enemies to scare them away from the troop!

FRUIT FANS

Chomp! A chimp bites into a juicy fig. Yum! This is the best forest snack.

Chimpanzees love to eat fruit! Figs are their favorite. They also munch on bananas, mangoes, and berries.

Chimps eat more than just fruit, though. They snack on leaves, seeds, and nuts. Sometimes they eat insects like termites and ants.

Chimps spend 6 to 8 hours each day looking for food. They remember where fruit trees grow. When fruit is ripe, they travel there to feast.

DID YOU KNOW?

Chimps eat hundreds of different kinds of plants! Even tree bark, flowers, and mushrooms.

CHIMP CHAT

FUN FACT!
Chimps can learn hand signals
from humans. Some have learned
over 300 signs!

Hoo hoo hoo! A chimp cups its hands around its mouth to call out loud.

Chimpanzees talk to each other in many ways. They use sounds, faces, and body movements. Each signal means something different.

Chimps make around 30 different sounds! A pant-grunt is used to say hello to leaders. A loud scream means danger. Some sounds can travel over a mile through the forest.

Faces tell stories too. A chimp with a big open mouth is playing. Lips pushed forward means it wants something. Chimps also use touch to share feelings. They hug, kiss, and hold hands to show they care.

WATCH OUT
DID YOU KNOW?
Leopards are excellent climbers and can follow chimps high into trees!

Rustle! A leopard creeps through the bushes. A chimp spots it and screams.

Chimpanzees have predators in the wild. Leopards are their biggest threat. These big cats hunt chimps at night and during the day.

Large snakes can be dangerous too. Big pythons may threaten young chimps.

Crown eagles are another danger. They may try to catch baby chimps.

Adult chimps are harder to catch. Their large size helps keep them safe. Staying high in trees also protects them.

STICK
TOGETHER

Whoosh! Chimps rush together in the trees. Safety in numbers!

Chimpanzees stay safe by sticking together. They travel in small groups. When danger is near, chimps talk to each other.

A chimp that sees a snake will make a soft "hoo" sound. If the danger is big, it makes a loud "waa" bark. This alerts the other chimps nearby.

If a predator gets too close, chimps work as a team. They scream, wave their arms, and throw sticks. Together, they can scare off enemies that one chimp could not face alone.

Chimps can run up to 25 miles per hour to escape danger on the ground quickly!

23

SWING TIME

Swoosh! A chimp swings from branch to branch. Its long arms help it reach.

Chimpanzees are amazing movers. They use their long arms to swing through trees like acrobats.

Chimps can also walk on all fours. They use their knuckles to support their weight, which is called **knuckle-walking**.

Sometimes chimps walk on two legs instead. This helps them carry food or see over tall grass.

Chimps can travel more than a mile through the treetops without ever touching the ground!

DAY LIFE

Yawn! A chimp wakes up in its nest as the sun rises.

Chimpanzees are busy during the day. They wake up early and start looking for food. Mornings are a great time to eat.

Chimps spend hours each day eating. They also rest during the hottest part of the day. During rest time, they groom each other.

Chimps pick bugs and dirt from each other's fur. This helps them stay clean. Before dark, they build new nests.

Grooming sessions can last over an hour. Chimps remember who groomed them and return the favor!

TROOP TALK

Squawk! A chimp greets its friends. The whole troop is together again.

Each Chimpanzee troop has its own territory in the forest.

Every troop has a leader, usually a strong male. Other chimps show respect to this leader.

Chimps know every member of their troop. They spend years learning who is who. Best friends sit together, share food, and help each other in arguments. Some chimp friendships last for life!

A troop can have up to 150 members, but chimps usually travel in smaller groups of 6 to 8.

FINDING MATES

Hoo hoo hoo! A male chimp calls out loud. Others listen nearby.

Chimpanzees can have babies at different times of year. This means there is no set mating season for them.

Female chimps are ready to have babies around age 13. Males are usually a bit older. Females often stay with the same troop their whole lives.

A female chimp has one baby at a time. Twins are very rare. She usually waits about five years between babies.

A mother chimp has only four to six babies in her lifetime. Each baby stays close 7–10 years.

CUTE BABIES

DID YOU KNOW?
A baby chimp cannot walk
until it is about 4 months old.
It depends on its mother for
everything!

Squeak! A tiny baby chimp holds tight to its mother.

Baby chimps are born with pink faces that turn darker as they grow. These tiny newborns only weigh about 4 pounds.

Babies cling to their mother's belly at first. Later, they ride on her back. They stay very close for the first few months.

Young chimps love to play. They chase each other and wrestle. Playing helps them learn important skills. Mothers nurse their babies for about 4 years.

They will often stay with their mother until they are teenagers. But their bond lasts for life.

MAMA KNOWS

Crunch! A mother chimp cracks open a nut. Her baby watches.

Mother chimps teach their babies important skills like how to find food and use tools. Young chimps learn by watching their moms closely. Then they copy what she does.

Moms carry their babies for years to keep them safe. A young chimp rides on its mother until age 4 or 5.

Mothers groom their babies every day. This keeps them clean and healthy. It also shows love and makes their bond very strong.

Mother chimps tickle their babies to make them laugh and play!

FORESTS FALLING

Crack! A tree falls in the forest. Chimps must find a new home.

Chimpanzees are losing their forest homes. People cut down trees for farms and wood. This is called **habitat loss**.

When forests shrink, chimps have less space. They cannot find enough food.

Hunting is another big problem. Even though it is against the law, it still happens. Chimps need our help to stay safe.

Only 170,000 to 300,000 chimps live in the wild today. They have lost 80% of their forest homes.

HELPING HANDS

A researcher carries a chimp back to the forest. The chimp is returning home.

People around the world work to save chimps. Scientists study them to learn what they need.

Some groups also protect forests so chimps have homes. Rangers guard chimps from hunters.

Rescue centers care for **orphan** chimps. Workers teach young chimps how to live in the wild again. A few chimps return to safe forests.

FUN FACT!

Jane Goodall has studied chimps for over 60 years. She also started a group to help keep them safe.

GLOSSARY

canopy
The top layer of a forest made by the leaves and branches of tall trees.

troops
A group of chimpanzees that live together.

orphan
A baby or young chimp that has lost its mother.

knuckle-walking
Walking on all fours with your hands curled into fists.

habitat loss
When animals lose their homes because people change the land.